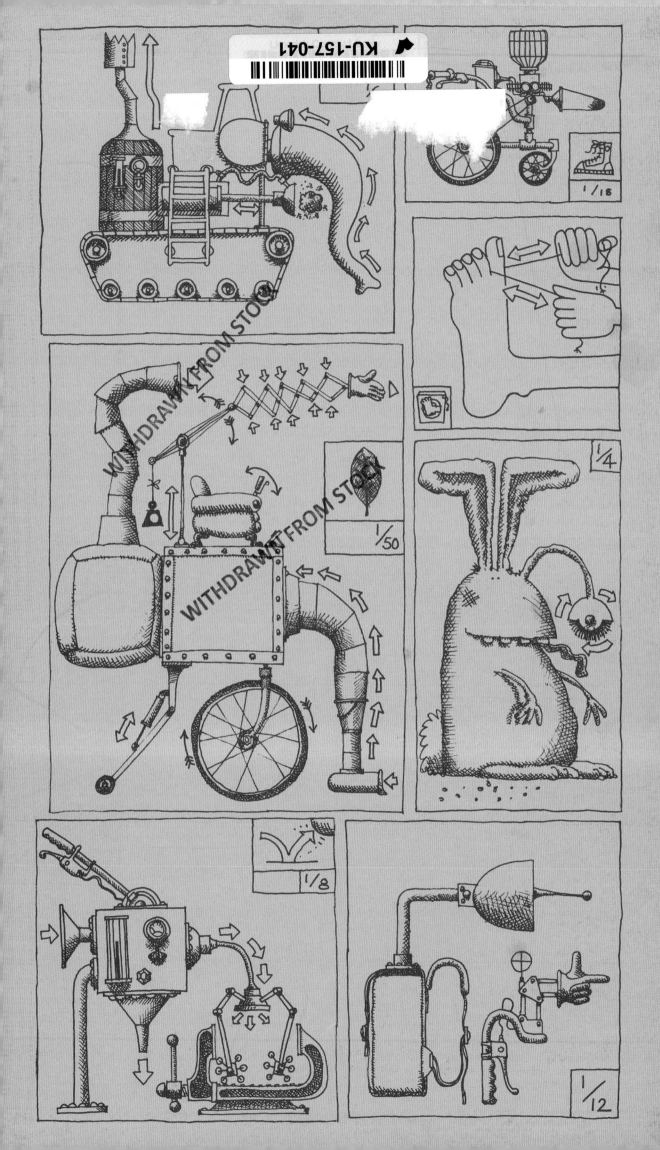

Stink Stoppers!

Stink
Stoppers!

(Ingenious Inventions for Pesky Problems)

Written by
Andrea Perry

Illustrated by
Alan Snow

Simon & Schuster
London

SIMON &
SCHUSTER

First published in 2003 in Great Britain by Simon & Schuster UK Ltd
Africa House, 64-78 Kingsway, London, WC2B 6AH
www.simonsays.co.uk

The text of this book is set in a typeface designed by Alan Snow.
The illustrations are rendered in pen and ink.
A CIP catalogue record for this book is available from the British Library upon request.

ISBN 0-689-83701-1

Manufactured in China

1 3 5 7 9 10 8 6 4 2

To Jordan and Dean,
my two most remarkable creations
— A. P.

To Annie and Isabel
— A. S.

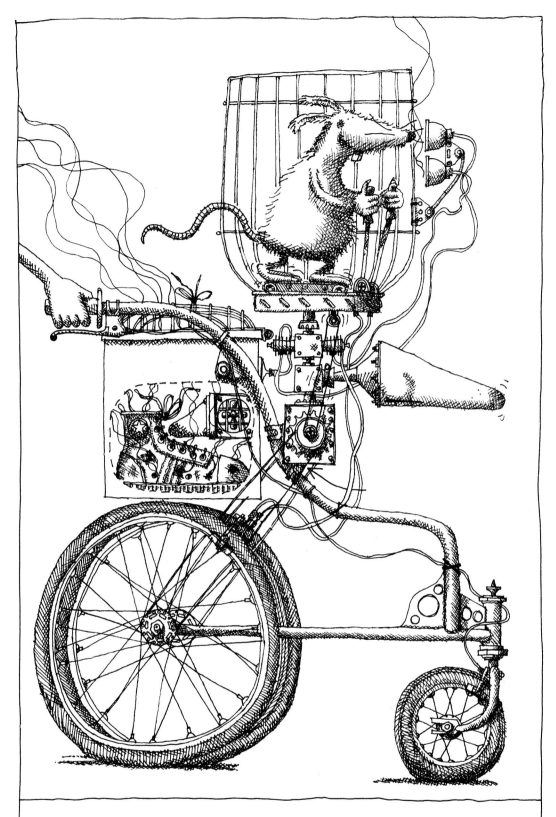

TABLE OF CONTENTS

THE SURE-FOOTED SHOE FINDER

How many times has this happened to you?
You're late for the school bus and can't find a shoe.
It might take you hours unless you have got
the Sure-footed Shoe Finder there on the spot!

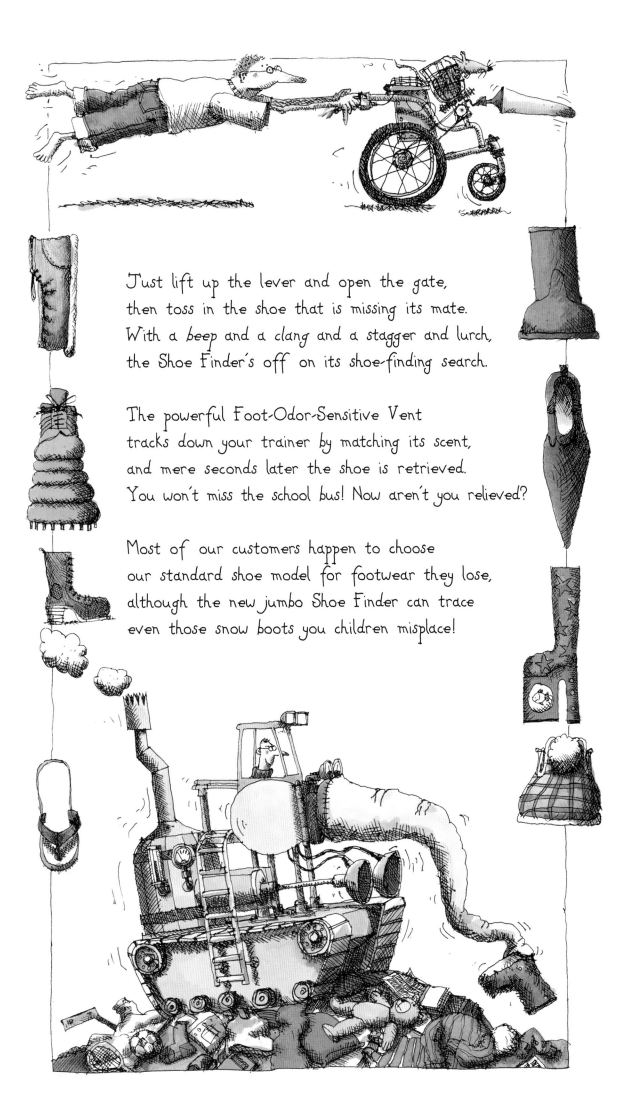

Just lift up the lever and open the gate,
then toss in the shoe that is missing its mate.
With a *beep* and a *clang* and a *stagger* and *lurch*,
the Shoe Finder's off on its shoe-finding search.

The powerful Foot-Odor-Sensitive Vent
tracks down your trainer by matching its scent,
and mere seconds later the shoe is retrieved.
You won't miss the school bus! Now aren't you relieved?

Most of our customers happen to choose
our standard shoe model for footwear they lose,
although the new jumbo Shoe Finder can trace
even those snow boots you children misplace!

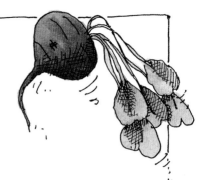

VEGGIES BE GONE!

"Put the broccoli back!" comes the cry from aisle four.
"We already have okra. Don't buy any more!"
"Please Mum!" the child begs, "I can't eat this stuff.
"Aren't cucumbers, eggplant, and turnips enough?"

Meanwhile in aisle number six you can see
a cart full of chips and a kid full of glee.
"How about ice cream?" the youngster proposes.
"Or three bags of Fruit-flavoured Chocolatey-ozes?"

The child back in aisle number six came prepared.
When he shops with his parents he never gets scared.
His cart has been treated with Veggies Be Gone!,
the produce repellent you simply spray on!

Its vapours prevent any artichoke heart
or endive from lodging itself in your cart.
Try buying some Brussels sprouts. Watch what they do:
They bounce right back out of your basket at you!

Say "So long" to spinach! "Good riddance" romaine!
Don't ever eat carrots or cabbage again!
New Veggies Be Gone! fends off beans, beets, and peas.
It even deflects cauliflower with ease.

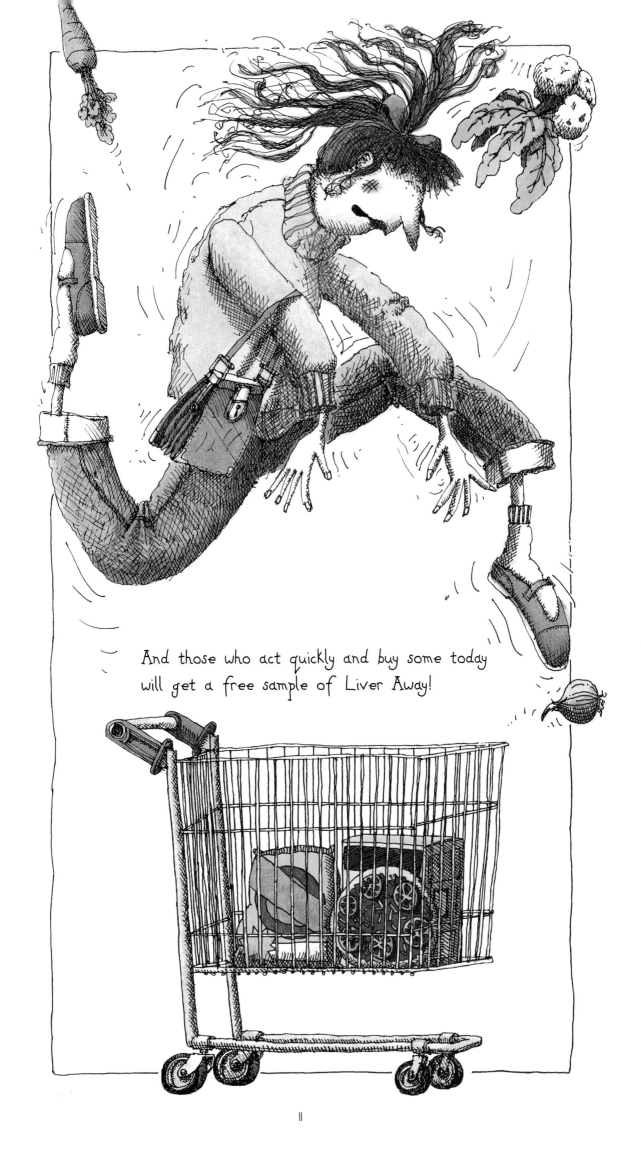

And those who act quickly and buy some today
will get a free sample of Liver Away!

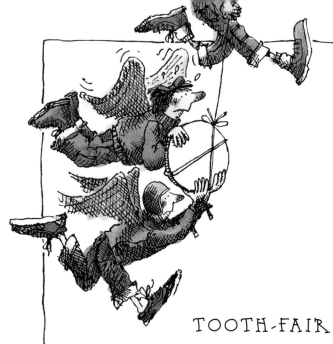

TOOTH-FAIRY FORKLIFT

Attention, Tooth Fairies:
Are you overworked?
Has the business of gathering teeth got you irked?
Don't bother with cheap pillow lifters and cranks,
with pulleys and levers and crowbars – NO THANKS!
Our Tooth-fairy Forklift
will hoist the tooth donor,
extracting the item
for sale by its owner.
Then quickly stick cash
where the cuspid had been,
insuring by morning
a big, toothless grin!
Our satisfied customers haven't stopped raving!
Imagine the time and the work you'll be saving!
It's never been simpler to have teeth removed. . . .
Get a Tooth-fairy Forklift, now new and improved!

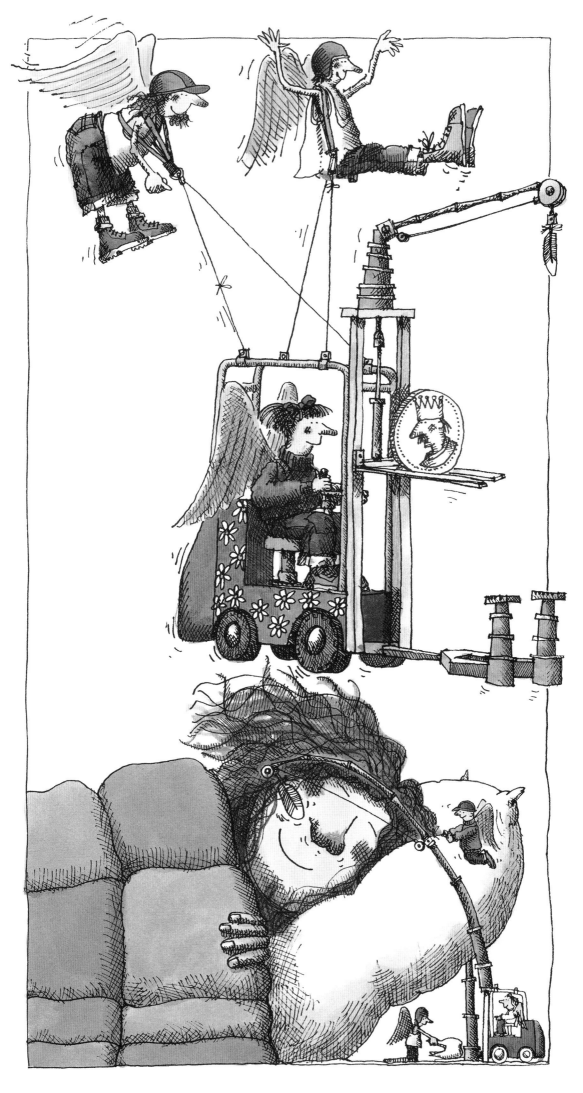

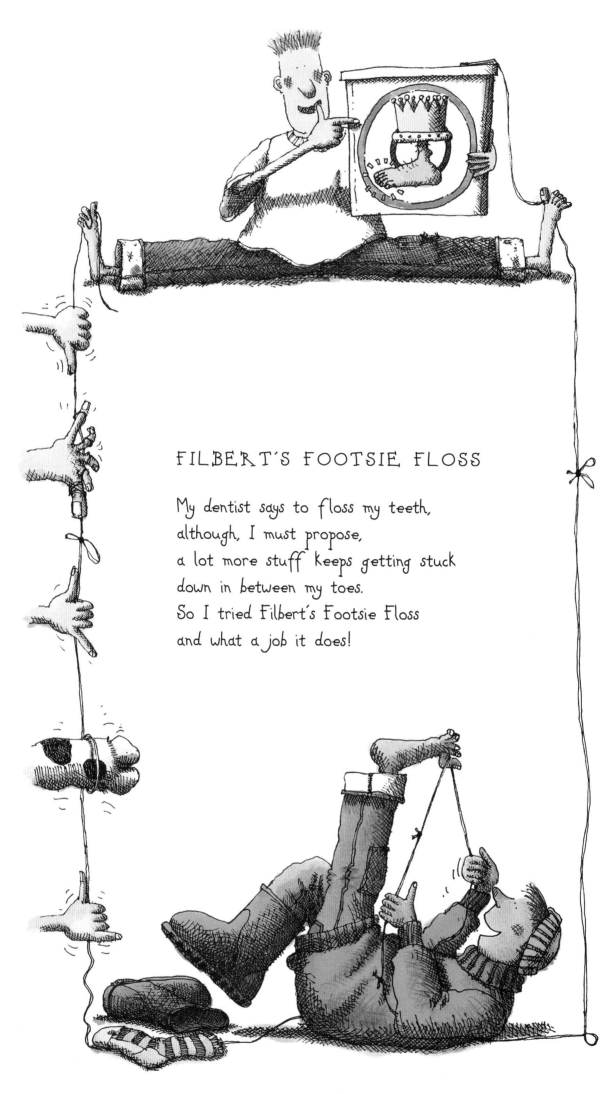

FILBERT'S FOOTSIE FLOSS

My dentist says to floss my teeth,
although, I must propose,
a lot more stuff keeps getting stuck
down in between my toes.
So I tried Filbert's Footsie Floss
and what a job it does!

Floss every night when socks come off
to help remove the fuzz!
Don't limit hygiene to your teeth –
give all your toes a treat!
Experience the cleanliness
that comes from fresh flossed feet!

STINK STOPPERS

Did you know you can hire a crew for your zoo
to get rid of animal odours for you?
A zoo visit's ruined when sea turtles stink,
or the caribou cage has a stench, don't you think?

We Stink Stoppers come in with lotions and hoses,
and extra tight clothespins to wear on our noses,
with sprays and with scrubbers, with cleansers and rags,
with brushes and sponges and zoo refuse bags.
Each creature's odour is pretty distinct,
but we fight those fumes until all are ex-stinked.

When pumas are putrid, we powder their paws.
Once eagles have eaten, we clean off their claws.
We bathe every bobcat, perfume every pen.
We wipe down each walrus again and again.
We brush tiger teeth and we trim hippo nails.
We shine and we polish each crocodile's scales.

Your yaks and your gnus can be sweet as a rose;
your pandas as pure as your big buffaloes.
The stench from your springboks can now be prevented.
Some days they'll smell spicy, and some lemon-scented!

We think you'll agree that it's better to choose
the service that only the finest zoos use!
Just call on our staff for a free consultation
of Stink Stopper Zoo Odour Elimination!

LEM LONNIGAN'S LEAF MACHINE

Lem Lonnigan's Leaf Machine cleans lawns with ease
by vacuuming all that falls down from the trees.
And as you might guess, he's quite busy in autumn.
Just look in a yard full of trees and you'll spot 'im!

He uses a special attachment to get
those few stubborn leaves that have not fallen yet,
extending its claws to reach sky-scraping heights
for snatching up stragglers and sometimes stray kites.

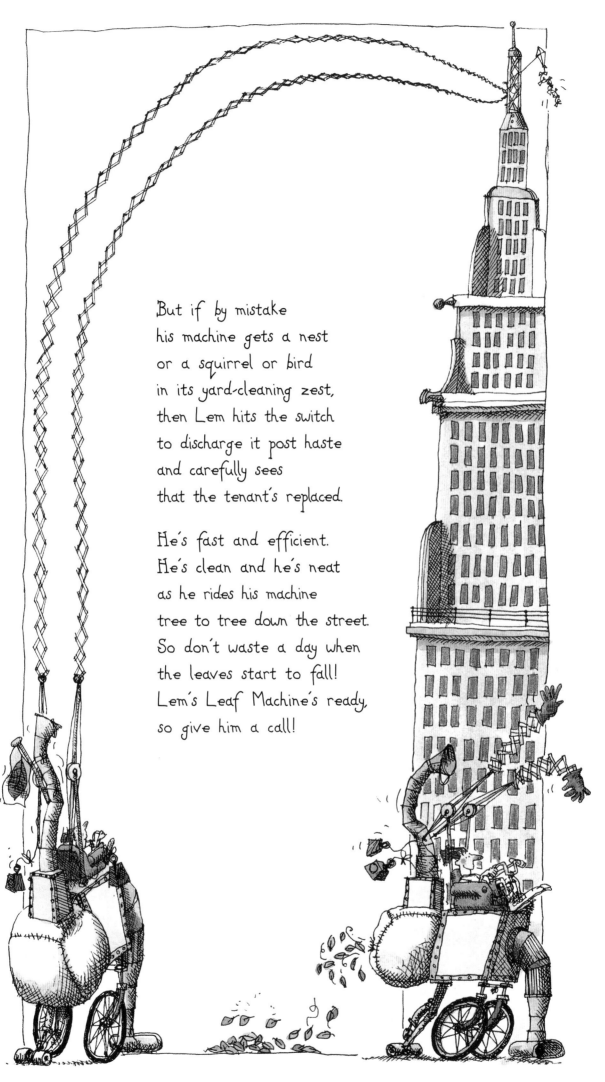

But if by mistake
his machine gets a nest
or a squirrel or bird
in its yard-cleaning zest,
then Lem hits the switch
to discharge it post haste
and carefully sees
that the tenant's replaced.

He's fast and efficient.
He's clean and he's neat
as he rides his machine
tree to tree down the street.
So don't waste a day when
the leaves start to fall!
Lem's Leaf Machine's ready,
so give him a call!

BILLY BOB'S BOUNCING BAZAAR

Why should all bounce be contained in a ball?
It doesn't seem terribly fair.
Why don't the dishes, if dropped on the floor,
bounce right back up in the air?

Accidents happen, no doubt about that,
but who are they happening to?
To people with fragile, unbounceable stuff,
and that doesn't have to be you.

Try shopping at Billy Bob's Bouncing Bazaar
where none of our merchandise chips.
Not one of our glasses will shatter or break,
in case a new customer trips.

We've suctioned the bounce out of rubbery balls,
inserted it into our mugs,
and then added more to our plates and our bowls,
and our vases and china and jugs.

So next time you fall while holding a plate,
make sure it's from Billy Bob's store.
All you'll clean up from your mishap will be
spaghetti and sauce off the floor!

ACME'S SUPER SPIDER SPOTTER

Every picnic situation
has a certain aggravation
due to its outdoor location.

Though the fresh air is enthralling,
even Muffets find appalling
all the spiders out there crawling.

That's why Mrs Muffet bought her
insect-fearing little daughter
Acme's Super Spider Spotter!

Super Spider Spotter metres
tell you within centimetres
just how close bugs are to eaters.

Then the Spotter Siren bellows
so all of those arachnid fellows
flee before exchanging hellos.

Picnickers need never fear it
even if they're very near it.
Only spider ears can hear it!

Curds and whey taste so delightful,
eating them need not be frightful.
Savour each and every biteful!

MAXIMUMBRELLAS

Maximumbrellas!
Maximumbrellas!
Perfect for on-the-go ladies and fellas!
What could be better
if you're in the rain,
running with luggage and late for your train?
Are you a musician
who carries a bass?
A student with books and a clarinet case?
A shopper with parcels?
A porter with bags?
A postal employee whose letter pouch drags?
When you've got your arms full
and need some protection
from bad weather coming in every direction,
Maximumbrellas
will travel beside you,
moving along as they cover and guide you!
They widen for wideness!
They heighten for highness!
They're fully equipped to give maximum dryness,
and can be adjusted
by setting the rollers
from "fast" for a jogger to "slow" for a stroller!

Maximumbrellas!
Maximumbrellas!
Perfect for on-the-go ladies and fellas!

SNUG-AS-A-BUG HOMES

So you've spotted
the Red-Speckled Flapdoodle Flea
asleep on a truffle-tree limb.
Don't shove the poor thing
in a Juneberry jar;
get a Snug-as-a-bug Home for him!

They come in all sizes
and styles and decors,
and the price range is moderate, too.
There's a Basic Bug Palace,
a Firefly farm,
and a Ladybug Lodge with a view.
There are Aphid Apartments
and Mansions for Moths
and some Condos for Crickets as well.

SAUNA

HOTEL

Massage!

There's even a Roach Ranch
with sauna and spa
next door to a Hornet Hotel.
Why the Early American Bee Bungalow,
with its honey-pot pool and high dive,
is quite a step up
if your last known address
was with six hundred drones in a hive!

While your bug is held captive
for class show-and-tell,
he deserves to be pampered a bit.
Why not show him you care
with an insect estate.
Gnat mite not be so bad now,
mite nit?

HEAVENLY HEIGHTS HITCH AND HARNESS

A short leash is fine if you're walking your dog,
your emu, iguana, chinchilla, or frog.
But what should you use so the neighbours don't laugh
when you're out for a stroll with your new pet giraffe?

The Heavenly Heights Hitch and Harness, of course,
for pets with an altitude higher than yours!
Or a pet with a neck that is rather extensive.
Our harness is sturdy and quite inexpensive.

If you've got a llama, alpaca, or camel,
or other such type of elongated mammal,
just fasten the harness and reel out the tether
so you and your loved one can travel together!

Safety in transit is our main intention
for creatures of virtually
every dimension!

CRUMBUNNY

This pet can't fetch, or swim, or sing,
roll over, catch, or anything.
He doesn't bark or beg — instead —
he eats the crumbs found in your bed!

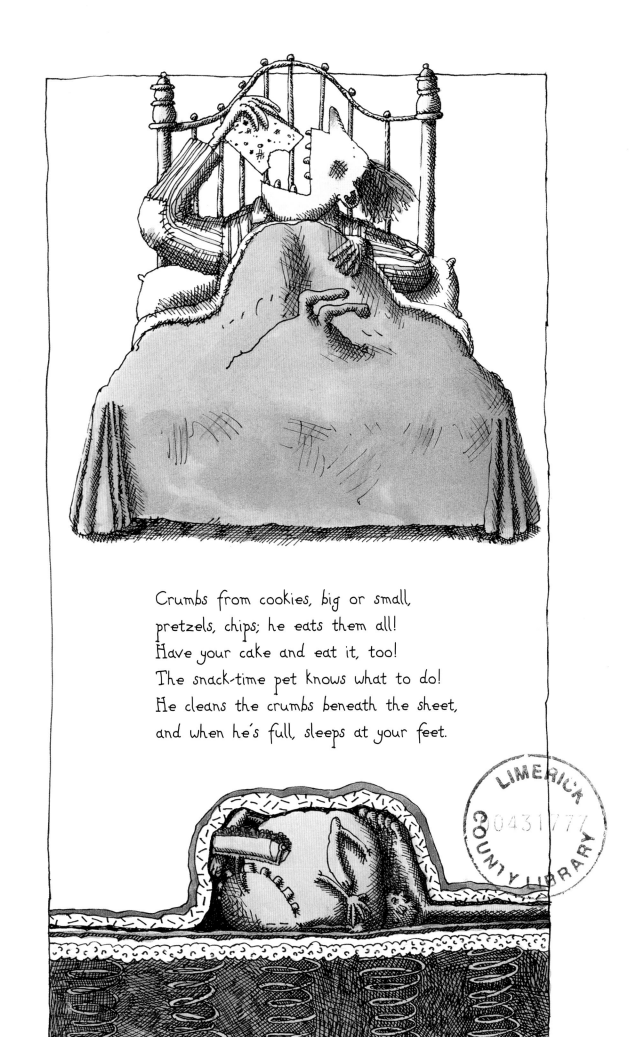

Crumbs from cookies, big or small,
pretzels, chips; he eats them all!
Have your cake and eat it, too!
The snack-time pet knows what to do!
He cleans the crumbs beneath the sheet,
and when he's full, sleeps at your feet.

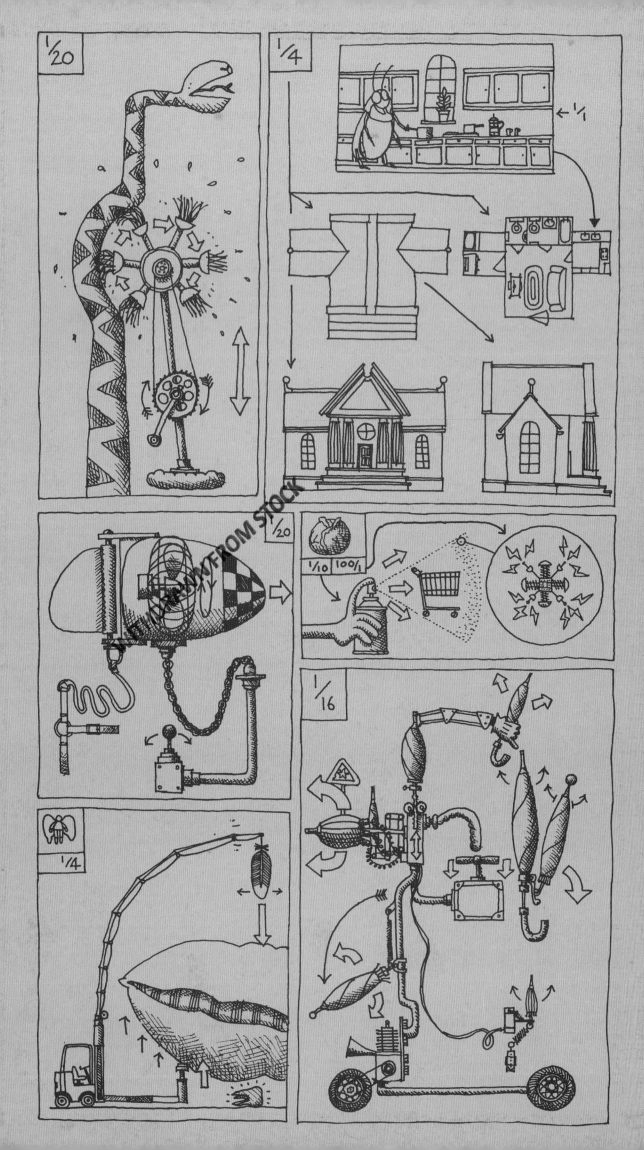